So What If I'm Single:
21 Ways to Maximize Being Single

ISBN 13: 978-1-7333593-0-6

Artwork By: Justin Hardin
Damascus Media

Edited By: Angela Edwards
www.PearlyGatesPublishing.com

HENRYLINDA
Publishing House
Atlanta, Georgia

Dedication

This book is dedicated to you for you from the inspiration of God through me. I hope you enjoy and are inspired to reach for your best life.

~ Louis ~

Table of Contents

Introduction

Understand this first: If you are single and are reading this book, you are single for a reason. Whether by choice or by force, there is a reason for it. Being single is not a curse upon your life, so don't be so hard on yourself. It is a great blessing. Being single is not just about preparation for your spouse, but preparation for your **life**. God, life, and the universe want you to take full advantage of your singleness. They want you to experience every great opportunity and blessing this world and life have to offer. You were born for a reason—***and a great reason at that.*** You may have been born to be single at this very moment just to inspire you to live better and conquer more than you would if you were married. However, most individuals forfeit this philosophy because they have been socially scripted and policed to think that a significant other or marriage is the optimal pinnacle in life, only to realize they have missed so many opportunities for success after they entered a relationship. So many people lay down their dreams, goals, and visions when they say, "I Do".

This book illuminates 21 ways and opportunities presented to you or created by you. So what if you are single! **Congratulations!**

Now, here is the disclaimer:

Let's be clear. This book is **not** the Bible. It is a book of wisdom nuggets and power tools for singles and all who desire to read it. It is simply comprised wisdom and facts to help advance not only singles but every reader who chooses to act on this wisdom. It is for everyone who chooses to gain knowledge on the playing field of their personal definition of success. Married, single, man, woman, young, old, all races, all nationalities, and all religions can profit from this book. There may be some advice in this book you may be fluent in, inexperienced in, or disagree with. Take from this book the wisdom you need to inspire you to be the best you.

Now, before you dive into this anticipated inspiration, I need you to do yourself a huge favor and make room for your future. First, ask for forgiveness from God, those whom you have wronged in the past, and those who have done the same to you. You are much bigger than the damage they caused. Then (and here is the most important thing), forgive yourself. Forgive yourself for everything you have done wrong and for allowing those who have done you wrong the opportunity to do it. You are much bigger than the damage you allowed. Clean your slate today. Take a deep breath and start off fresh. It's never too late to start over. You may not be able to start over with the same thing or person, but you can always start over. You may have failed at some relationships and opportunities, but there will be more to come and presented.

Learning from your previous mistakes and bad decisions may be more valuable than not making them at all.

Make absolute peace with them. One of the funniest, most popular comedians originated the following quote:

"I was who I was. I am who I am. And I'm cool with both of them."
~ Steve Harvey ~

Learn from your mistakes, make peace with them, and release yourself from them. **Unlearned lessons from past failures will restrict your openness to think about future opportunities.** Don't embrace the bad from your past. You don't have to cling to them just because you made them. Take advantage of your new opportunity to not just make things right, but GREAT! You now have the opportunity to engage in the best life possible for you. Here are a few opportunities you can engage in starting today that will prepare you for the next and "new" you:

- If you don't know it, find your purpose. You are much more valuable than having a spouse and family.
- Educate yourself. Learn more so you can earn more.
    "Formal education will make you a living;
    self-education will make you a fortune."
    ~ Jim Rohn ~
- Read, read, and read more.
    "Rich people have small TVs and big libraries,
    and poor people have small libraries and big TVs."
    ~ Zig Ziglar ~
- Become direct and upfront in conversations and decisions.
- Learn the value of time itself, your personal time, and time management.

- Build your vocabulary. Learn a new language.
- Learn how to say "no" to people.
- Live without limits. You should have none.
- Volunteer.
- Set objectives and become goal-oriented.

This book is for you and about you. **See you on the other side of the new you.**

FREEDOM

If you are single,

Learn Who You Are and Why You Exist.

Many people have yet to understand this point. Do you know who you really are? Do you understand why you were born into existence? Do you know your purposes and passions to fulfill in this life? Have you learned how to discover your purposes *(if you don't know them)*? Even though learning about yourself is a lifelong journey, strike out to discover who you are and why you are here—and embrace both. That is a must for a successful, holistic life. Knowing and operating in your passions and purposes can help lead you to financial success and also the right spouse suitable for who you are.

"What we really want to do is what we are really meant to do. When we do what we are meant to do, money comes to us, doors open for us, we feel useful, and the work we do feels like play to us."
~ Julia Cameron ~

So, the question remains: ***Do you know how to find them?*** Shannon Kaiser wrote an article for the Huffington Post on ways to discover your purpose. Following is some of what she had to say:

"Many of us struggle because we try to find that ONE thing that we are meant to do; but trying to find only one thing is the reason why we feel like something is missing. The notion that we have only one thing we are meant for limits us from fulfilling our greatness. Take me, for example. I have six different job titles. I'm a Life Coach, Travel Writer, Author, Speaker, Teacher, Mentor, and Designer; and each thing I do brings me joy, but none of these are my purpose—they are my passions. So, start getting in touch with your passions! When you lead a passionate life, you are living your life on purpose.

"Let go of thinking there is only one purpose for you and embrace the idea that our purpose in life is to love life fully by putting ourselves into our life! This means we jump in and try new things; we stop resisting the unknown and we fully engage in what is happening right here, where we are. To lead a purposeful life, follow your passions. When we live a passion-filled life, we are living on purpose, and that is the purpose of life.

"That feeling that something is missing goes away when you lead a passion-filled life. The need to seek our purpose comes from the lack of passion. When you don't feel connected to your life, you lack purpose and passion. To fix this emptiness, simply add more passion. To boil it down, remember this simple equation:

Passion + Daily Action = Purposeful Life

"Consider that the real purpose of anyone's life is to be fully-involved in living. Try to be present for the journey and fully-embrace

3

it. Soon, you will be oozing with passion, and you will feel so purposeful and fulfilled, you will wonder how you lived life without it. Enjoy the journey into your own awesome life."

It's hard for anyone to learn who you really are if you are having a difficult time learning about yourself. There is so much attraction towards an individual who fully embraces the competence of who they are. It is highly suggested that you know who you are because you don't want to be with someone who is compatible with either **who you used to be or who they think you should be**. Make sure your mate or potential mate can satisfy the intangible needs of not only where you are, but where you are going. One of the worst mistakes in choosing a mate is to be with a person who cannot identify with nor articulate your intangible necessities *(emotions, conversation, chemistry, and capacity to love and handle you)*. The Proverb ***"Do not be unequally yoked"*** will forever stand strong as a universal axiom. The more mature a person becomes, the more a person is stimulated and attracted to the conversation, dialogue, and discussion.

Being attracted to a person physically highly-stimulates for a short time. However, the mind has the ability to stimulate and sustain a relationship for a lifetime.

So, make sure the conversation is mutual and reciprocal. When it comes to choosing a spouse, take the mind over body any day.

"People never learn anything by being told;
they have to find out for themselves."
~ Paulo Coelho ~

Learning who you *are* will help you learn who you are **not**. Don't waste any more precious seconds of your life being a person you are not. Don't inquire about it, think about it, or entertain it. It should **NEVER** be an option. If a person of interest is asking you to be who you are not, he/she should **NEVER** be an option as a potential mate. You have to understand the *intangible* value of your life. Your life should not have an option for purchase with the entire world's combined currency to persuade you to be who you know you are not. Your standards are your standards. Your morals are your morals. Hold fast to them. Someone will come along who will value them just as much as you do.

"Good judgment comes from experience, and experience comes from
bad judgment."
~ Rita Mae Brown ~

If you are single,

Enjoy You and Your Life.

Have a balanced life. Live a balanced life. Successful individuals do not have work on their agendas all the time. They set aside time for their families *and* themselves. Consider it a way of recharging your batteries. If you are always buried in a pile of work, you are missing out on life. Personal time is critical because it's the time you're able to review your life and where it is headed. That is the time you reflect and develop new strategies for your success journey. The day-to-day regimen of successful people is not that hard to master. Anyone may do it, though not everyone has the proper *mindset* to really see it through.

Learn to stop and enjoy moments. There are some moments that are therapeutic. Those moments come only for you to recognize them, acknowledge them, and genuinely receive them. They come to make you happy and have enjoyable experiences. Those moments know that you need them at that given time. Stop. Take a second. Pull out your listening ear to hear what those moments want to tell you. There is something they want you to learn and take with you as you travel this road called 'life'. Learn to celebrate your life and life itself in those moments.

"I believe that the greatest gift you can give your family and the world is a healthy you."

~ Joyce Meyer ~

In addition, I suggest using this free time to enjoy traveling. Go and enjoy all of nature's beauty and beautiful scenery on this earth. If you woke up tomorrow and decided to attack your Bucket List and travel to Australia to snorkel in the Great Barrier or stroll down the ancient streets of Venice, your significant other would likely feel some type of way if you traveled without them—and rightfully so, especially with such short notice. **BUT** when you're single, you have the freedom and flexibility to travel without reservation and reluctance.

Why wait until you're in a committed relationship or married to explore the life you want to experience? If you're totally single, you honestly don't know when you will meet a potential mate, let alone marry. That can be a long wait! By the time you marry, you may not have the opportunities to travel to some places. Take advantage of the opportunity **now**.

Following is a portion of some statistics from the New York Times on traveling singles:

"...some 24 percent of people traveled alone on their most recent overseas leisure vacation, up from 15 percent in 2013, according to the 2015 Visa Global Travel Intentions Study, which was

conducted across 25 countries by Millward Brown, a market research organization. Among first-time travelers, solo travel is even more popular, jumping to 37 percent, up from 16 percent in 2013."

There is so much to learn from different places on this earth. Traveling helps to become progressive and relevant with diversity. Learning new cultures, languages, customs, traditions, etc. can even help develop a non-traditional relationship that will never know what boredom is. There is so much more that can be learned from a person who is full of diversity. That kind of diversity is attractive to many people. Who knows? You may meet your future mate while you're traveling!

"The man who goes alone can start today, but he who travels with another must wait till that other is ready."
~ Henry David Thoreau ~

If you are single,

It's OK to Wait. You Don't Have to Rush.

You may be in your 20s. *You still have time.* You may be in your 30s. *You still have time.* You may be in your 40s. *You still have time.* You may be in your 50s. *You still have time*...but not as much. **I'm just joking.** But seriously, studies now show that more people are waiting until after their 30s to marry or become seriously involved with someone. Waiting until the age or time of maturity increases the chance of having a more successful relationship.

How about some more truth? Go and pursue some things. Don't allow the fear of being alone sabotage your season of being single. God will give you the grace to be single and handle it well. Become the best **YOU**. Become the person you desire to marry. Focus on your career. Become successful in a craft. Make your name great in an industry and/or field.

Build your best name to leave your best legacy.

This takes time, experience, sacrifice, and more. It's a part of the process. An online blog by Next Shark had this to say about singles who wait until later in life to desire relationships:

9

"After you've reached a good point of success in your life, you will have taken in so much experience on building and managing something that you'll find that you can apply these same concepts to your love life. While your friends that got married in their 20s are now all divorced and depressed that they wasted the last couple years of their life instead of building themselves, you'll have people drawn to you because of your success. You'll know how to properly manage your relationships and you'll be strong enough to fall back on yourself if things don't work out. Remember: The more successful you are, the more options you have. Make your finances and career a top priority. I don't care what you've been taught. Having financial stability is incredibly important. As one of my old mentors said, "Without money, you ain't (nothing)!" This is the hard truth and don't let anyone else tell you differently. If you're spending time on finding or maintaining a relationship, that means you are wasting time that you could be spending on making yourself financially stable. The last thing you want to do is work on a fairytale relationship only for it to end badly because you'll be left with nothing but a broken heart and nothing to fall back on."

"Being single is when you can say what you want, do what you want, whenever you want, and wherever you want."

~ Anonymous ~

If you are single,

Get Rid of the Baggage.

How often do you spring clean and declutter? Do you like your home neat and tidy with space or chaotic and disorganized? Do you normally stay on top or ahead of your business or do you allow things to pile on top of each other and *then* take care of them? Many people handle their relationships like they handle their business and priorities (or lack thereof).

In getting rid of your baggage, you must be brutally honest about the things that make up the content. You need time and stillness to ponder and identify all of what they are. Sit down and make a list of the things that can potentially hinder the healthy progress of a new or existing relationship. Take responsibility for all of them. This is an important step.

**If you don't admit ownership of your baggage,
you won't consistently work to discard it.**

Even if life or people have influenced the baggage, it is still your responsibility to discard it or recycle it into a new form. No one is going to do this for you. This is your responsibility for your personal and relational development. Only you know what is deep down in the depths of your soul that is a major hindrance. No other human being knows you better than you. You know you at your best **and** worst. Even if you find a mate *(or a mate finds you)* before you correct your baggage, at the right time, you owe it to that person to sit them down and inform them of the things about you that you are making a committed effort to change. That person will have the choice to leave or stay; but on most occasions, they develop a greater respect for you because of your honesty and commitment. It encourages them to share their baggage as well. It also encourages both of you to genuinely assist each other with those changes. This may help create a strong bond in the relationship.

In a classic hit song called *Bag Lady*, famous R&B singer Erykah Badu expresses one of the most profound verbal metaphors to articulate the adverse complexity of harboring baggage. One of the stanzas in the song says:

Bag lady you gon' hurt your back
Dragging all them bags like that
I guess nobody ever told you
All you must hold onto, is you, is you, is you.

One day all them bags gon' get in your way
One day all them bags gon' get in your way
I said one day all them bags gon' get in your way.

12

One day all them bags gon' get in your way, so pack light,
Pack light, mm, pack light, pack light, oh ooh.

Bag lady you gon' miss your bus
You can't hurry up, 'cause you got too much stuff
When they see you coming, [brothers] take off running
From you it's true, oh yes, they do.

One day he gon' say you crowding my space
One day he gon' say you crowding my space
I said one day he gon' say you crowding my space
One day he gon' say you crowding my space so, pack light
Pack light, mm, pack light, pack light, ooh ooh.

Erykah uses metaphorical euphemisms to nuance a universal narrative about the adverse effects of baggage. Her point to relay is that many people don't like to deal with individuals for too long who have too much baggage. It takes too much work and requires a lot of energy to deal with. They would rather be single with peace than to be married or in a relationship with chaos. Truth be told, **all** people have baggage, but not everyone does "spring cleaning" frequently. They live their lives as hoarders, piling everything into small spaces. People who like to live in peace don't like to feel claustrophobic. This conclusion suffocates relationships and brings them to a demise. Make the decision to live life with as little baggage as possible. Make the decision now.

"When people clean house, they resolve old conflicts."

~ Cate Perry ~

If you are single,

Own Your Own Happiness.

You have to **have** and **own** your own happiness. You are responsible for it. No other human being is responsible for you having that gift. Notice the word *"have"* is used instead of *"be"*. To 'have' is to possess, own, or hold. To 'be' is to exist, occur, or take place.

Before anyone can be anything, that person must have ownership of that particular thing first.

So, your happiness in its totality must be outright **owned** by you. No one should be able to purchase your total happiness. No one should be able to sell you theirs, either.

Here is the deal: If you rely on people (i.e. a spouse or significant other) or circumstances to give you complete happiness, you will never receive the completion. They may *make* you happy, but they can't *keep* you happy. They don't have the capacity to maintain it. It would cost them their happiness to complete yours. If that happens, their happiness will suffer because they are giving all their happiness to you. That will cause the relationship to suffer because you have neglected to maintain your own. You must 'have' in possession your own happiness to help balance your life and the lives of others closest to you.

How do you own your own happiness? You must know the things that make you happy and maintain a healthy balance of them. If exercising, music, attending social events, pampering, shopping, sports, or specific hobbies make you happy, take ownership of them. They play a substantial role in the balance of a healthy mentality. The key is to not neglect but maintain a healthy balance, even after marriage or entering a relationship. Just make sure these things are morally-sound and will not compromise or jeopardize your integrity or the integrity of the relationship.

The next two points about owning your own happiness may be the most important:

1. When a significant other *(or people in general)* walk into a person's life, both parties should enhance each other's happiness; not fulfill it. Both parties must allow and grant each other freedom to possess his or her own happiness. In other words, a person cannot choose the way another person wants to possess their happiness. Allow them their freedom to maintain what sustains their healthy balance in life. If anything needs to be changed in their life, it is not your job to do it. Both parties must secure the trust of each other regarding happiness by giving freedom to express it in its fullness.

2. You must also embody your happiness. Google's definition of *embody* means *"to become an expression of or give a tangible or visible form to (an idea, quality, or feeling)"*. In other words, to embody something is to make what is invisible visible. You give it a body of some form to overtly reveal and express who or what it is. When a person embodies their happiness, it attracts people. It is contagious and infectious because it's magnetic. It can bring the best out of the worst of people. Daily, many people live a mundane lifestyle because embodied happiness is not their normality. However, people are electrified in the presence of an embodied, happy individual because that person brings so much energy to the atmosphere.

You will also give your relationship a huge advantage by embodying your happiness. Your mate or spouse will always want to be around you because of the magnetic energy you bring. Many people greatly-desire that kind of elemental atmosphere in their relationship but can't seem to get it to shift. It's because someone or both parties are not embodying their own individual happiness. People want to be around individuals who give positive energy; not steal it. Many relationships with great potential are short-stemmed because of the non-existence of overt happiness. A person who embodies much of their happiness lives in search of a potential mate—one who can reciprocate what they give. In a hit song called *You Make Me Wanna,* famous pop star and icon, Usher Raymond, said it best:

"You make me wanna leave the one I'm with, start a new relationship with you, this is what you do."

Even though that is actually a daily occurrence in many relationships, we can minimize the chances of a relationship "turnover" by practicing the embodying of our happiness through who we are. Take your happiness, own your happiness, and embody your happiness. The birth of others embodying their happiness may happen through the overt expression of yours.

"Success is not the key to happiness. Happiness is the key to success. If you love what you are doing, you will be successful."

~ Albert Schweitzer ~

FUTURE

If you are single,

Would People Pay Top Dollar for Your Service or Skill Set?

Is there something you have to offer to the world? Is there something you have that can boost the world's economy? What about something that will positively change the culture of a society? Is there something the world has been waiting on for decades and you have it locked inside of you? We are waiting for you to arrive! We need you! We need what you have! And we need what you have to be *developed*. There are people waiting and willing to give you what you ask for in exchange for what they need from you. But in order to receive paramount medium of exchange, your skill must be developed and perfected.

Give yourself some time to develop your experience with your skill set because the experience must contest with the competence of what you have to offer.

Build the confidence in yourself by building
the competence of your craft.

This comes through the consistency of building a great work ethic. Competence will always remain an attraction agent for desired compensation. However, many times, your experience and efficient finesse determine your altitude of exposure and compensation that you assert. Developing your skill set will always play a key role in the escalation of your success. Are you spending time *on* you to develop your service and/or skill set? Do you believe that you can be what you see in others? Do you believe you can become what you and others have never been?

You must do what you've never done to gain what you've never had. But, you must first become who you have never been to go where you've never gone.

That is the key. Live by that aphorism. Also, learn the following verb and brand it into your subconscious: **INVEST**.

"An investment in knowledge pays the best interest."
~ Benjamin Franklin ~

Invest. This word is one of the most underrated words to engraft into one's innate philosophy and culture. The Cambridge English Dictionary's definition of *invest* is *"to put money or effort into something to make a profit or achieve a result"*. You **MUST** invest in yourself and into your craft or skill set.

Consumer spending stimulates nearly 70% of the U.S. economy and, according to Trading Economics, Consumer Spending in the United States averaged 5,319.31 USD Billion from 1950 until 2017, reaching an all-time high of 11,839.70 USD Billion in the second quarter of 2017 and a record low of 1,320.40 USD Billion in the first quarter of 1950. But what would happen if half the currency the consumers spent was on investments for themselves and their future? How much more advanced would society be? How much boost would be stimulated in the economy? What about the national debt that could be remunerated? Similar to other countries, costs such as healthcare and secondary education would be free; but that only comes when individuals perfect their service or skill set, capitalizing and monetizing the opportunities presented because of their perceptive value they possess.

So, invest in yourself!

The most valuable, tangible entity you should value is YOU.

That doesn't mean you're narcissistic, but rather that you understand the success of your endeavors reposes entirely on you. They cannot grow or flourish without your growth. Network, educate yourself, build relationships, and take care of your totality. Now, ask yourself this question: "*At this moment, would I receive what I believe I'm worth?*"

"Money is a reward for solving a problem for others."
~ Dr. Mike Murdock ~

If you are single,

Arrive.

L et's take a look at the life of one of the greatest humanitarians and anti-war activists, Mahatma Gandhi. Gandhi was a trailblazing and prolific leader who practiced law and advocated for Indian civil rights of Indians in his homeland, India, and South Africa. Known for his preliminary liberation movements and boycott formations against British rule, he is also considered the engineer of the beginning non-violent—yet defiant—civil rights movements that would influence other significant world leaders to follow suit. Even after his demise, Gandhi's commitment to passive resistance has been an inspiration of hope for oppressed and ostracized people worldwide. His philosophy, Satyagraha (policy of nonviolent resistance), will forever rest as one of the most effective philosophies in independence movements around the world. His actions enthused future civil rights movements worldwide, including those by civil rights leaders Martin Luther King, Jr., James Luther Bevel, and Nelson Mandela.

Let's make sense of this. Could it be that if Gandhi had never answered the call of his purpose and arrived at the occasion of racial oppression, world humanitarian leaders such as Martin Luther King,

Jr., James Luther Bevel, and Nelson Mandela would not have had a blueprint to read or paved road to travel on their journey of civil rights? Could it be that a humble man from India, which is approximately 8,400 miles away from the United States, would build a non-violent civil rights prototype that would unquestionably affect the civil rights of other ethnicities, nations, and gender? He had no clue that his culture and life would be a model to reshape the dynamics of civil society. He had arrived at his destiny and pursued it.

With that being said, is the world waiting for **YOU** to arrive? Is there a society, generation, policy, legislation, culture, idea, economy, etc. that will be reformed because of the principles and culture you express through your life? There are many individuals who watch us and are being impacted daily. Our lives make their lives better. In their eyes, we have arrived at their occasion to help them become better. Even the greatest leaders had some form of mentorship to help lead and scale them to be who they have become. We have sons, daughters, family members, friends, loved ones, associates, colleagues, etc. and people whom we will never meet who are waiting for us to arrive at our place in destiny and purpose. That is why having a sense of urgency is imperative. Whether you envision yourself as a minute or immense social influence, your influence matters. Your experience matters. Your voice matters. Your support matters. **YOU MATTER.** You matter so much that the divine gifts bestowed upon you cannot be administered to society unless you share them. You have been given the wonderful opportunity to bring substance to someone's life in some form. Don't wait until marriage to invoke change into society.

The longer you wait to invoke change, the longer the people whom you will influence remain stagnant.

You just may be holding them back by procrastinating. Arise and arrive! Become the answer to a future question…the solution to a future problem…the return for a future investment…the renaissance to an absent generation. There is a generation who cannot see their promise land until you awaken to your purpose and expose it to them. Arise, I say—**and arrive.**

"What did you bring to the table? I brought the table to the table."
~ Bishop RJ Matthews ~

If you are single,

Excuses Shouldn't Stop You.

L isten. Level up and move now. This is the opportunity for you to get in the game. The rubber must now meet the road.

"Opportunity is missed by most people because it is dressed in overalls and looks like work."
~ Thomas Edison ~

Following is a true story about an individual who realized excuses are averse to success. It is an extensive, yet profound, article from Wikipedia on the early life of this individual:

"After her birth, her mother traveled north and she spent her first six years living in rural poverty with her maternal grandmother, who was so poor that she often wore dresses made of potato sacks, for which the local children made fun of her. Her grandmother taught her to read before the age of three and took her to the local church, where she was nicknamed "The Preacher" for her ability to recite Bible verses...

"At age six, she moved to an inner-city neighborhood in Milwaukee, Wisconsin, with her mother Vernita, who was less supportive and encouraging than her grandmother had been, largely as a result of the long hours she worked as a maid. Around this time, her mother had given birth to another daughter, Patricia who later (in February 2003, at age 43) died of causes related to cocaine addiction. By 1962, her mother was having difficulty raising both daughters, so this individual was temporarily sent to live with her father, Vernon, in Nashville, Tennessee. While she was in Nashville, her mother gave birth to a third daughter who was put up for adoption and later also named Patricia. This individual did not learn she had a second half-sister until 2010. By the time she moved back in with her mother Vernita, her mother had also given birth to a boy named Jeffrey, her half-brother, who died of AIDS-related causes in the 1980s.

"This individual has stated she was molested by her cousin, uncle, and a family friend, starting when she was nine years old. At 13, after suffering years of abuse, she ran away from home. When she was 14, she became pregnant, but her son was born prematurely, and he died shortly after birth. She began going to Lincoln High School; but after early success in the Upward Bound program, was transferred to the affluent suburban Nicolet High School, where she says her poverty was constantly rubbed in her face as she rode the bus to school with fellow African-Americans, some of whom were servants of her classmates' families.

"She began to steal money from her mother in an effort to keep up with her free-spending peers. She would lie to and argue with her mother. And she would go out with older boys. Her frustrated mother once again sent her to live with her father, Vernon, in Nashville, Tennessee, though this time, she did not take her back. Vernon was strict, but encouraging, and made her education a priority. She became an honors student, was voted Most Popular Girl, and joined her high school speech team at East Nashville High School, placing second in the nation in dramatic interpretation. She won an oratory contest, which secured her a full scholarship to Tennessee State University, a historically black institution, where she studied communication.

"At the age of 17, this individual won the Miss Black Tennessee beauty pageant. She also attracted the attention of the local black radio station, WVOL, which hired her to do the news part-time. She worked there during her senior year of high school, and again while in her first two years of college. Working in local media, she was both the youngest news anchor and the first black female news anchor at Nashville's WLAC-TV. She moved to Baltimore's WJZ-TV in 1976 to co-anchor the six o'clock news. In 1977, she was removed as co-anchor and worked lower profile positions at the station. She was then recruited to join Richard Sher as co-host of WJZ's local talk show, People Are Talking, which premiered on August 14, 1978..."

The world now knows that individual as one of **the most** powerful entrepreneurs and self-made billionaires in the world.

Having a net worth of approximately $2.9 Billion (Forbes, 2016), Oprah Winfrey is one of the greatest and most profitable actresses, directors, and producers in history. She has definitely accomplished incomparable success through origination and revolution to create her own wealth. She understood that excuses could not exist in her world in order to be successful. She had to find inspiration and motivation to endure.

Find and keep your motivation. Find a ***reason*** to keep your motivation. Truth be told, we all have excuses that could legitimately justify procrastination, suspension, or disembarking of something— but here's the deal about excuses:

1. ***Excuses are like A**holes: We all have at least one; and***
2. ***They are rational, according to circumstances.***

Per Google, an *excuse* is *"a reason or explanation put forward to defend or justify a fault or offense"*. But it gets deeper... Google **also** says that excuses are *"often reasons put forward to conceal the real reason for an action"*. That's the real deal truth. In Latin form, *excusare* means *"to be free from cause or blame"*. Are you using daily excuses to not venture into your desires, responsibilities, and endeavors? What are you afraid of? What is your Goliath? Are you afraid to fight for your success?

If it doesn't give you a reason to fight Goliath,
you have already lost.

With excuses, you will always live with the consequences of untapped potential, opportunities, and skills you possess. You will never know all what life has to offer you by making excuses. A few of the top issues of fear are: fear of failing, past mistakes, embarrassment, lack of competence, lack of confidence, the unknown, and lastly, even success. Fear is a real issue but actually, it doesn't exist. It is such a paradoxical phenomenon. Fear is only an *emotion* that causes one to believe that danger, a threat, or pain is near. Since emotions don't have a physical body and cannot be seen, we can be assured that emotions only exist in the mind, which we all have full control of. Fear can be fully-absorbed and/or eradicated.

To eliminate excuses from our lives, we must first eradicate fear. It's okay to feel the fear. Do it. Feel it. Yes, you may not have a legitimate excuse, but do it anyway; **BUT** don't allow something as minute as fear or an excuse stop you from going forth. IQ Matrix provides 11 types of excuses most people make, and they are undeniably accurate:

1. There is not enough time.
2. There is not enough money.
3. I don't have the education.
4. I'm too young or old.
5. I don't know how.
6. I can't change.
7. I'm afraid to fail.
8. It's not the right time.

9. I have to plan thoroughly.

10. It just won't work.

11. I'm not inspired.

If even **ONE** of those listed excuses is standing between you and your desires, remove it. Remember: *Fear comes from an emotion and an excuse comes from a circumstance.* They will continue to remain the deadbolt that has your door to opportunity locked. You are greater than any fear. You are better than any excuse. Go forth!

"Courage is being scared to death but saddling up anyway."

~ John Wayne ~

If you are single,

You Belong at the Top with the Rest of Them.

Who told you that you can't? Who told you that you have to wait? Who told you that you have to ask? Who told you that it was impossible? Who told you that weren't qualified? Who have you been consulting with? Who has been speaking into and over your life?

Can we switch gears for a second? Why **not** you? Why **can't** you be next? Why **can't** you be the next millennial boss, CEO, president, entrepreneur, leader, etc.?

If your faith can see it, your effort can manifest it.

You possess the power to live in the clouds. You possess the power to build your own kingdom. You possess the power to belong at the top. Humans were built with God-like features. If we can believe, we can do. The human mind is the breeding ground for evolution, revolution, innovation, creativity, and so much more. We have the power to think and then create. We are the only beings that have these capabilities. That's why animals operate instinctively only. They only know how to survive within their domain. However, their domain is very limited. This condenses their ability to be creative and change. Since you have the power to change, your only obstacle is **you**.

A changed mind is a changed life.

Get out of your own way and get to the top. Your destiny is waiting on you. Grow your faith in yourself by stretching your faith in yourself.

"A mind that is stretched by a new experience can never go back to its old dimensions."
~ Oliver Wendell Holmes ~

You were made to succeed. You were meant to do the impossible. You were created to dream, envision, and manifest. When God envisioned and created this earth and mankind, He gave us the perfect blueprint on the importance of believing in ourselves to execute the blueprint we mentally see. He knew He could because He believed He could—and you must know you can…if you believe you can. You were placed on this earth to build, encourage, and leave your physical expression of faith. The physical expression of your faith is the visible manifestation you make. People will believe you when they see what you have done. You were made to produce what you mentally see and it becomes a success. Mankind was made to become and grow into success. We were built by God to never remain constant, but to accelerate in the continuity of the evolution of time. This world does not operate in the antiquity of its primitive stage. It has advanced throughout time with technology and innovation. However, it takes individuals who push the envelope of faith to stamp it with action. It takes an individual who is not afraid to conquer. You were, in fact, born to conquer. You were born to win. You were not made to fear **FEAR**. However, there are levels to this thing.

Being a conqueror and conquering are experiences, but being a champion is a **lifestyle**. A champion is someone or something that has won a contest or competition. This takes hours of preparation, training, and experience in winning. It takes winning many battles or conquering many conquests before you can lay claim to the title of "champion". In other words, it takes *time* to develop a champion.

A champion is not just born...but developed.

You were born with the proclivity to conquer, but you must be trained to be a champion. It's great to be a conqueror, but more rewarding to be a champion. Allow your experiences as a conqueror to develop the champion in you. It will change your trajectory, lifestyle, and culture to be wired to succeed in everything you do.

Have you ever read the success story of Colonel Harland Sanders, Founder of KFC (Kentucky Fried Chicken)? When he was eligible for social security, he was furious when he received a check for $105.00! He started KFC at the young age of 65. Yes, 65! He lived out of his vehicle traveling the country while attempting to sell his recipe to other restaurants. It is unbelievable how many times he received a "no" before he got his first "YES". **1,009 times!** Not to mention, but he became a billionaire by age 88. That's extreme faith!

What about Walt Disney? Once fired because he was told he lacked imagination, he was rejected **309 times** by banks before he received funding for Disney World. That, too, is extreme faith!

Getting cut from his junior high basketball squad, Michael Jordan said, *"I have missed more than 9,000 shots in my career. I have lost almost 300 games. On 26 occasions, I have been entrusted to take the game winning shot, and I missed. I have failed over and over and over again in my life. And that is why I succeed."* That is why he is considered one of the greatest basketball players and businessmen of all time. He has extreme faith! There is a life you have never imagined on the other side of **your faith.**

Become a great leader and strive for excellence. A great leader has the power to inspire confidence in others and move them to action. They possess the ability to efficiently and effectively direct, delegate, communicate, and solve problems. A leader also learns how to have emotions, but not be emotional when resolving issues. Inc.com lists the following seven keys and their descriptions on how to become an exceptional leader in the workplace. They can also be applied universally:

1. **Delegate wisely** - Possess the competence to effectively delegate both the responsibility for completing assignments and the authority required to get things done.

2. **Set goals** - Every employee needs their own individual organizational goals to strive for. Set specific and measurable goals with your employees, then regularly monitor their progress toward achieving them.

3. **Communicate** - You must make every effort to get employees the information they need to do their jobs quickly and efficiently.

4. **Make time for employees** - Put your work aside for a moment, put down your smartphone, and focus on the person standing in front of you.

5. **Recognize achievements** - Every employee wants to do a good job. And when they do a good job, employees want recognition from their bosses.

6. **Think about lasting solutions** - No matter how difficult the problem, there is always a quick solution… But we often overlook the lasting solution that may take longer to develop. The next time you have a problem to solve in your organization, deal with the cause of the problem instead of simply treating the symptoms.

7. **Don't take it all too seriously** - Without a doubt, running a company is serious business… Successful leaders make their organizations fun places to work. Instead of having employees who look for every possible reason to call in sick or to arrive

to work late or go home early, organizations that work hard and play hard end up with a more loyal, energized workforce.

Inc.com has great knowledge on gaining the right momentum to becoming a great leader!

Here is a statement that should be embedded in your mind:

You are an asset, not a liability.

Change your thinking. Being a single individual should never be a liability. You should always be an asset. As a matter-of-fact, mankind started off being an asset. According to the Bible, man's first responsibility was to take care of the earth. He was to be an asset to the economic efficiency of the earth. An *ASSET*, not a *LIABILITY*.

An *asset* is *"a person, thing, or quality that adds value"*. Whatever you pursue should appreciate in value. In pursuing excellence, being an asset is a requirement…a prerequisite. It should be innate and second nature. Many people view being single as condemnation, judgment, a death sentence, or even an illness. However, in order to adopt the culture and concept of living as an asset, you must change your thinking about yourself.

Anything that appreciates in value is self-aware of its value.

It knows how much it is worth, and value is always asserted with credibility. Here is the deal with credibility: It is one of the simplest (yet most powerful) characteristics one can possess. To be credible is to be reliable, integral, and trusted.

To display the characteristics of being credible is to perfect the astuteness of being an asset.

Life has enough hands that take away possessions. Be one of the few hands that give.

"The question isn't who is going to let me;
it's who is going to stop me."
~ Ayn Rand ~

If you are single,

Get Up Early.

It doesn't matter what people say, the early bird will **always** get the worm. Most successful individuals rise early in the morning. Why? Because the earlier you start your day, the more time you have to accomplish your tasks or goals for the day. Rising early helps you mentally prepare for the entire day and its challenges. If you take an individual who arises two hours before work and an individual who arises 20 minutes before work, you find that the one who arises two hours before is more mentally prepared for the day. Take advantage of the early rise by reading, studying, exercising, meditating, praying, brainstorming, planning, etc. Along with proper rest and pre-planned days, you will find rising early helps to foster more of a productive day.

"My formula for success is rise early, work late, and strike oil."

~ JP Getty ~

Arise before the rising of the sun and command your day. Conquer the day before the day begins. Your mind is clear, your spirit is alert, and you are not troubled by the matters of the day. That doesn't mean nothing adverse will occur during the day, but it does mean that the day cannot control you and your emotions. You have power. Your words have power. **REAL power**. Humans are spirits living in a physical body. However, our words are just as real as our bodies are!

Did you know that you can bless or curse your possessions, plans, and your own life subconsciously and not know it? According to Wikipedia, Masaru Emoto (a Japanese author, researcher, photographer, and entrepreneur) claimed and proved that human consciousness has an effect on the molecular structure of *water*. Emoto's conjecture evolved over the years, and his early work explored his belief that water could react to positive thoughts and words, and that polluted water could be cleaned through prayer and positive visualization.

Exercising early in the morning helps to stimulate focus for the day and helps improve the overall totality of the body. A study conducted in 2013 by *Health Psychology* shows that happily-married couples are more inclined to gain weight within the first four years of marriage, proving the complacency to one another about their appearance. Single people tend to be more health-conscious for the sake of the right impression from a prospective partner. A study was found by *Psychology Today* that collected data of approximately 13,000 Americans, ages 18 to 64. It concluded that single men exercised 8 hours, 3 minutes in a two-week period while the married men exercised 4 hours, 47 minutes within the same two-week period. Single women also exercised 5 hours, 25 minutes during this period. Married women exercised for 4 hours. Even though the average man exercises more than the average woman, single individuals are proven to exercise more than married individuals.

True wealth starts with health. Many individuals who have a high value for their health have a high value for their life in general. Exercise certainly is a portion of the day-to-day regimen of successful individuals. It will make you feel good about yourself, keep the body healthy, keep the mind alert, and teach you discipline. As a matter-of-fact, over half of successful business individuals discover a way to exercise each day. If you cannot exercise in the morning, get it in around lunch time or in the early evening. If you are on the ground floor and are traveling to the fifth floor, take the stairs rather than the elevator—but do not overexert yourself because it may set you back. You must make exercising a **habit**.

"The only bad workout is the one that was never started."

~ Unknown ~

If you are single,

Become and Remain Pliable.

L et's go to school for a moment. There is a scientific term called *homeostasis* that is very synonymous with remaining pliable. Included here is a perfect scientific definition and understanding from Dictionary.com that will help articulate the interrelation between the two:

Homeostasis *(hō'mē-ō-stā'sĭs)*
"The tendency of an organism or cell to regulate its internal conditions, such as the chemical composition of its body fluids, so as to maintain health and functioning, regardless of outside (external) conditions. The organism or cell maintains homeostasis by monitoring its internal conditions and responding appropriately when these conditions deviate from their optimal state. The maintenance of a steady body temperature in warm-blooded animals is an example of homeostasis. In human beings, the homeostatic regulation of body temperature involves such mechanisms as sweating when the internal temperature becomes excessive and shivering to produce heat, as well as the generation of heat through metabolic processes when the internal temperature falls too low."

Let's now discuss. The body is built to immediately and instinctively adapt to a sudden change in temperature, climate, environment, culture, etc. Now, let's make this applicable to daily living. Can a person maintain mental, psychological, and spiritual homeostasis when external life events happen? Can one quickly adapt to a sudden event and keep going? This is easier said than done. Most individuals find it hard to remain in a state of expandability and adaptation, whether it is voluntary or involuntary. What happens when the career of 10 years comes to a sudden close, a debilitating accident happens, unplanned divorce, the death of a loved one, sudden relocation, bankruptcy, or some other financial crisis occurs? How will you handle the pressure and reality of the change? How will you adapt? Will you stand and remain in a state of mental shock? Or will you be able to quickly adapt to the sudden change that life has abruptly presented to you?

There is an indefinable placed called *"in between places"* that will cause an individual to ask the following two questions: ***"How did I get here?"*** and ***"Where do I go from here?"*** Often, we think that what we do or the relationships we have is who we are. And whenever what we do or the relationships we have come to an end, we automatically think our lives have come to an end as well. This period of redefining can be tough work, but life doesn't have to end because of an event, circumstance, or situation. You are not defined by what happens to you.

You are not limited to a mere moment in your life.

43

You are larger than anything that happens in your life. That is why it is dangerous to become a slave to a career, business, spouse, goal, or anything futile or finite. To remain pliable at your core is to remain in control of your destiny. Before you were born, you were given instincts to adapt to life at any given moment. Many individuals don't utilize the full potential of their instincts. Many focus on social scripting and performance rather than their innate instincts to adapt and conquer.

Your instincts are just as powerful as your influences.

"Living by instincts elevates your ability to know where you are going and how to get there. It can help you know when to slow down and step back and when to accelerate and step up. And it can ultimately guide you to what you're looking for."

~ T.D. Jakes ~

Your outcome in life isn't up to a single individual; it's up to **YOU**. Remain adaptable to any situation in life. It will always give you an advantage of transitioning at any sudden moment. Train yourself to develop a homeostatic mind and trust your God-given instincts. Training is required because it is not intrinsic. Many individuals do not trust their God-given instincts, making adapting to life harder than what it may appear. This extends periods of an indeterminate state that was meant to only last for a very brief period of time. Whether it is a change of careers or from a sudden divorce from a 10-year marriage to stepping back on the dating scene, remain one who has the mentality of the appearance of the chameleon. Your colors can change with any surrounding. Pliable individuals learn and know who they really are and how far they can be extended based on their ability to adapt. Remember: **You are not what you do, but you are who you are.**

"It's how you deal with failure that determines
how you achieve success."
~ David Feherty ~

If you are single,

Become Organized and a Planner.

One thing most men learn about most women is this: *Women love a man who can plan.* Most women desire a man who can lead and be authoritative, not a tyrant. Great leadership requires planning, and people don't mind following a person who is a great leader. Life is a lot easier for those who learn to develop organizational planning skills. It also says a lot to a person you are dating, courting, or married to. They understand you are living a purpose-driven life. They have a proclivity that you know who you are, where you are going, and have no time for games. People who are great organizers and planners can quickly perceive when they are wasting someone's time or if someone is wasting theirs. Make this characteristic a priority while you are single. It has a vast array of ambiguity that is helpful in not just relationships, but life.

Also, create a daily task list. Objectives are important, but not more than executing the tasks to reach the objectives. Not attaining goals may lead to a lack of self-worth and depression. However, executing daily tasks help boosts you towards the person you wish to become. Long-lasting success is built into your daily routine of executing a daily task list. **If you show me a person's daily routine, I'll show you a person's level of success.**

In order to be successful, you have to be proactive. Being proactive requires a person to always be ahead. Creating daily task lists helps to build a proactive system, one that fosters productivity. Most people produce a system and create their daily tasks days in advance, or at latest, the night before. Success is always integrated with systems. This is an acute step in building sustainable, provisional success. If you plan to be successful with something specific, it starts with your daily routine. Your daily routine starts with your daily tasks lists. Whatever the tasks may be, successful people start and finish the work, perfecting their competence in execution.

"By failing to prepare, you are preparing to fail."
~ Benjamin Franklin ~

If you are single,

Build a Brand.

What are you known for? When people see you or hear your name, what is their first thought of you? Is everyone's thought of you the same? It's very important to build a personal brand for yourself in your single state. Do you plan to build a business? Make a name for yourself? Climb the corporate, social, and/or economic ladder? Have you ever attempted to assemble anything without the proper tools? Yes, I'm sure you were efficacious in building a few items. But you also noticed you could've been more efficient with your time had you had the proper tools.

The same applies to personally branding yourself to efficiently accomplish your goals. Personal branding is the process people use to differentiate and articulate themselves from their competitors. Branding identifies and markets what makes you different and what makes you stand out from others in the market. People should be able to associate your name with something great, positive, uplifting, relentless, relevant, etc. You are a brand. You are a business. Your brand **IS** your business.

When people meet you or speak to you, would they purchase *YOU* as a product?

That is why you must carry yourself as a walking and existing business. You should treat yourself as the hottest product on the market. You must sell who you are and who you are will sell your brand. Research how to efficiently and efficaciously brand yourself both personally and professionally. Every moment you spend investing and embodying your brand efficiently will always bring a natural reward.

"If people like you, they will listen to you;
but if they trust you, they'll do business with you."

~ Zig Ziglar ~

FINANCE

If you are single,

Budget and Save Your Money.

I t is so important to keep up with your finances. Yes, the euphoric impression that two incomes for the financial building of one household sounds majestic. Here is a hard fact: Many people go broke from relationships and the financial negligence associated with them. According to the 2010 Consumer Expenditure survey, single people spent on average $34,471 while married individuals without children only spent $28,017. In total, singles now spend $1.9 trillion every year in the United States. These numbers increase annually. The survey proves undisciplined financial practices to be frugal among singles.

Many relationships and marriages have failed because of the lack of finances, poor budgeting, or neglect of financial literacy for a couple. Relationships cost money. Gifts, wining and dining, and dates are **NOT** free. Unless you come from a place of financial freedom and stability, a relationship may not be wise to pursue and may add more fuel to the fire of your economic stress. Without a great understanding, it's difficult to work another full- or part-time job *AND* maintain a successful relationship. We all have the same 24 hours in a day's span. Breaking those hours into very small portions to give to a relationship is unacceptable to most individuals on the receiving end and rightfully should be understood. However, if working an additional job or your current job is demanding of most of your time and compensates well, understand that the opportunity to meet your goal of saving money may be the advantage over a relationship. What good is a relationship without adequate time to develop and nurture prudently?

Remember this: Your money is your money. It is widely said among the married community, *"What's mine is mines and what's theirs is mines"*. Even though this may be a truth among the betrothed, that doesn't apply if you are single. You may have certain goals to attain that may cost time and money. Set a goal of the amount needed to save and give yourself a space of time to save it.

Unless someone comes along and is worth the interruption of your plan, discipline yourself not to date anyone during this period.

One thing that most singles neglect is an emergency fund. A rule of thumb is to have **at least** six to nine months' wages saved in case anything happens. This needs to be kept in a high interest-bearing account—one you can access liquid cash without penalty. Do you have a six to nine months' emergency fund? Having one definitely says much about the level of discipline a single person has when it comes to their finances. This makes a difference to some individuals who are screening for a mate. However, the more money you have, the more options in dating you have. That is a fact. So, don't consume your mind with the notion that you can't do better than your past relationships or opportunities to date. There are a plethora of single individuals who have done what you are doing. They are waiting for someone like you to rise to their occasion. Don't be afraid to save your money and attain your goal.

Wait. Let's address the *'35 and Under Club'*. The rapport with this age group and saving and consumerism is becoming more and more detached. Here are known summarized truths: Technology has afforded the ability to compare prices and deals and shop online. However, the lack of discipline in consumerism is exposed through the practice of minute frugal behavior and rise in impulse buying. Following is a great corresponding article from one of the best-known online business journals, Gallup.com:

"Americans use a variety of methods to handle saving or spending money. With a few exceptions, Gallup discovered that across six different polling periods, millennials were more likely to have engaged in most of the spending and saving behaviors asked about than were members of other generations. These findings present something of a paradox, however, because some of the behaviors are less thrifty than others. On the thrifty side of the ledger, around seven in 10 millennials have gone online to compare prices (71%), while this is true of more than half of other generations (55%)...

"Millennials and older generations are equally likely (84%) to have purchased generic or store-brand goods. But while the

percentage of millennials purchasing generic or store-brand goods increased over the past year, it declined by three percentage points among the older generations. Finally, older generations used coupons while shopping more often than millennials (60% vs. 55%)—the only cost-saving method to show that pattern. Coupon use declined among all generations over the past year. On the spending side of the ledger, millennials are more likely to engage in a number of less thrifty behaviors, suggesting they might be a little more freewheeling with their spending than are members of other generations. They are much more apt to have gone shopping for fun, to have made an impulse purchase, and to have made a major purchase that cost at least one week's pay than are members of the other generations."

What a great article by Gallup.com! Although consumerism is available at society's fingertips, it has opened a portal to spend more impulsively. Consumers need to be more cautious of the access of spending and more conscious of the reserve of capital.

"A budget is telling your money where to go
instead of wondering where it went."
~ John C. Maxwell ~

If you are single,

Establish Good Credit and Pay Off Bad Debt.

Get ready to become enlightened. You will be reading this section for a while. Now, this is important. Ask yourself this question: *"Is it fair for your future spouse to pay for your poor credit history?"* That is exactly what can happen if you have poor credit or no credit at all when entering into marriage. Try your best to pay off derogatory debt such as collections, closed accounts, etc. Debt can damage your future, even if you marry a person with excellent credit. Remember this truism:

You can own a high credit score.

But a low credit score will own you.

That is why successfully caring for credit is one of the most important—and can be detrimental to decisions one can make.

Do you know your current credit score? When was the last time you pulled your credit report? Do you know what accounts are listed on your credit report? If you do not know any of this information, stop reading this book and go find out...**NOW**. In this age in the finance and lending world, your credit is who you are. It tells whether or not you and your word can be trusted. With the fast pace of the economy, it doesn't have the time to listen to you. It listens to your credit.

Cash is the king, but credit is the power of the king.

Much of this country is under fire and huge financial constraints because of poor financial decisions involving credit. Poor credit scores can be a result of poor credit decisions. Having a poor credit score increases the chances of a poor lifestyle. A poor credit score costs more in the long run than an excellent score. For example, a person with a 750 credit score will save thousands of dollars more in interest and principal than a person with a 600 credit score. Individuals with a high credit score receive very low interest rates, more room for negotiation of price, and the best rebate rewards for satisfying credit scores. Contrary to high scores, individuals with low scores receive the highest interest rates, less bargaining room, and little to no rewards for derogatory credit. Credit is so powerful that it controls much of an individual's livelihood. Poor credit can halt a person from getting a great job, living in their dream home, purchasing a nice car, halt a business opportunity, etc. There are so many personal endeavors in an individual's life that are adversely affected by having poor credit. Again:

The economy doesn't listen to you; it listens to your *credit*.

The economy views credit as a human being standing alone on its own two feet. If your credit is poor, the economy treats it poorly.

However, if kept in great standing, your credit will be respected with high regard wherever it goes.

Your credit can take you places where your cash cannot.

Establishing and building credit while single is such a pivotal work. Even though building the ethics of credit is such a vast and demonstrative task, there are basics that the average consumer should be abreast of as it relates to the knowledge of credit. Your credit score can be your best friend or worst nightmare. It wants to help you but can be the death of a dream if abused. A bad credit report from abused credit decisions results in a poor credit score. Your credit score is not your credit report. Your credit score is comprised of multiple factors from your credit report. According to an article on the basics of credit from Forbes.com, here are those factors:

- *35%: Payment history. This one is simple. Just pay your loans and credit card bills on time.*
- *30%: Amounts owed. This has to do with something called your 'Credit Utilization Ratio'. Essentially, you don't want to be using a high percentage of your total available credit. For instance, instead of maxing out your credit card, aim to spend no more than 30% of your credit limit.*
- *15%: Length of credit history. Generally, the longer you've been using credit, the better.*

- *10%: Credit mix. It's best to have a variety of accounts, including revolving debt (like credit cards) and installment loans (like mortgages).*
- *10%: New credit. Refrain from going overboard and applying for a bunch of new loans and credit cards in a short period of time. It looks like you're desperate for credit.*

Let's sample more basics on credit that educates all individuals:

- Your credit score indicates your creditworthiness to lenders. Your credit report lists the entirety of your credit history with creditors that report to the credit bureaus.
- The credit score range is from 300 to 850. The higher the score, the better range of credit in lending you may possibly be granted. The difference between a FICO score of 620 and 750 can often be tens of thousands of dollars over the term of a loan. A low score can cost you money each month. Good credit is commonly considered a 700 score or above.
- There are three major credit bureaus: Equifax, Experian, and TransUnion. All three determine their own three separate scores and three separate credit reports.
- By federal law, you can obtain one free credit report per year from all three credit bureaus by visiting www.annualcreditreport.com. There is an additional fee for your credit score. You can also visit www.MyFICO.com to

view your credit score for a fee. Also, your credit is not affected if you pull your own credit report.

- Give yourself time to establish and/or fix your credit. It won't happen overnight. It can take years to build great credit, but it's worth it to be patient.
- Too many inquiries from creditors will decrease your score. Be wise in applying for credit.
- Pay your bills on time and more than the minimum payment.
- Learn the difference between good and bad debt.
- Your FICO score is not the only credit score. Some lenders use VantageScore, the score from the credit bureaus themselves. There are also different versions of these scores. Sometimes, the credit score you see is not the same score lenders calculate.
- Monitor your credit reports throughout the year. There may be errors or fraudulent activity found on your reports. It is up to you to get those issues corrected. Don't be afraid to dispute an issue with either of the three credit bureaus.
- Most mortgage companies use the middle score of the three credit bureaus. According to FHA.com, applicants applying for Federal Housing Administration mortgages in 2017 are now required to have a minimum FICO score of 580 to qualify and a 3.5% down payment. If your credit score is below 580, a 10% downpayment is required.
- Conventional mortgage companies and banks usually require a minimum 620 credit score. Individuals with a credit score of 740 or higher usually get the best interest rate.

- There are ways individuals with no credit can build credit for the first time. Apply for a secured card or other credit card considered for people with bad or no credit. Department store credit cards are not strong builders for credit. Maintain a low balance with each card, become very frugal with your spending, and make more than the minimum payment on time. A rule of thumb is to keep the balance of each credit card under 30%. You can also become an authorized user on someone clse's crcdit by thc individual adding you to his/her account. If that individual is responsible and has built good credit over time, this will help boost your score quickly. However, they'll be ultimately responsible for any debts you incur. Keep that in mind. There are also some companies that will help you get loans based on your payment history for rent and/or utilities.
- You can negotiate terms, interest rates, payments, etc.
- Closing credit cards with great payment history can hurt your credit.

Understand this last thing about credit: Credit is an Equal Opportunity for everyone. Your race, gender, ethnicity, economic status, etc. doesn't matter. Everyone has the same opportunity to build excellent credit. There are individuals who are in the tax bracket of "below poverty" and have a 750 credit score. They live within their means but would qualify for just about anything they desire— according to their credit score. There are individuals who make six figures yearly and have a 580 credit score. Until they build their credit to match their income, their ability to finance using their credit is limited. So, they must use cash (which costs more than using credit). There is no credit bureau only for the rich or only for the poor. Your credit is just like the World Wide Web. It doesn't care about the status of an individual. So, be wise and safely leverage your credit, maintain a low debt-to-income ratio (less than 30% recommended), buy a home, own an appreciating asset, start a business, establish business credit, invest your money, etc.

"If you think nobody cares if you're alive,
try missing a couple of car payments."
~ Earl Wilson ~

If you are single,

Build and Establish Wealth.

Y ou do not have to be a financial genius to be wealthy. It's actually quite simple. There are no secrets. The success behind wealth-building is conservatism and time. You must give yourself space to allow both to mature through your plan. Develop healthy daily habits to save and diversify your money to build wealth. This requires discipline, strategic planning, time, and execution of your goals. It's not anything clever, ingenious, or super-creative. Reduce your spending. Increase your savings. Increase your earnings. Increase your investments. There are many ways to establish and build wealth. Investing in compounding interest-yielding investments and accounts, real estate investing, starting a business, etc. are some examples of ways to build and establish wealth.

Invest in the economy. Take advantage of a growing economy by investing in the stock of growing companies. As the economy grows, so does a company's revenue. That's because economic growth creates earnings. That increases buyer demand, which drives more revenues into companies' cash registers. In other words, when people spend money, businesses make money. What better way to make money than from the returns on investments from investing into a growing company? **Allow your money to make more money!** With the convenience of technology, purchasing shares of stock is relatively easy compared to years ago. You can purchase shares through a broker, brokerage firm, a financial planner, online brokerage, or directly from the company. Not only is it easier to purchase investments, but there is a plethora of ways to invest your money. Of course, to decide which investment vehicles are suitable for you, you need to know their characteristics and why they may be suitable for a particular investing objective. Following is one of the most simplified yet informative articles on investing 101 and the different types of investments from Investopedia.com:

BONDS. Grouped under the general category called 'Fixed-Income Securities', the term "bond" is commonly used to refer to any securities that are founded on debt. When you purchase a bond, you are lending out your money to a company or government. In return, they agree to give you interest on your money and eventually pay you back the amount you lent out.

The main attraction of bonds is their relative safety. If you are buying bonds from a stable government, your investment is virtually guaranteed, or risk-free. The safety and stability, however, come at a cost. Because there is little risk, there is little potential return. As a result, the rate of return on bonds is generally lower than other securities.

STOCKS. *When you purchase stocks, or equities, as your advisor might put it, you become a part owner of the business. This entitles you to vote at the shareholders' meetings and allows you to receive any profits that the company allocates to its owners. These profits are referred to as 'dividends'.*

While bonds provide a steady stream of income, stocks are volatile. That is, they fluctuate in value on a daily basis. When you buy a stock, you aren't guaranteed anything. Many stocks don't even pay dividends, in which case, the only way that you can make money is if the stock increases in value—which might not happen.

Compared to bonds, stocks provide relatively high potential returns. Of course, there is a price for this potential: You must assume the risk of losing some or all of your investment.

MUTUAL FUNDS. *A mutual fund is a collection of stocks and bonds. When you buy a mutual fund, you are pooling your money with a number of other investors, which enables you (as part of a group) to pay a professional manager to select specific securities for you. Mutual funds are all set up with a specific strategy in mind, and their distinct focus can be nearly anything: large stocks, small stocks, bonds from governments, bonds from companies, stocks and bonds, stocks in certain industries, stocks in certain countries, etc.*

The primary advantage of a mutual fund is that you can invest your money without the time or the experience often needed to choose a sound investment. Theoretically, you should get a better return by giving your money to a professional than you would if you were to choose investments yourself. In reality, there are some aspects of mutual funds that you should be aware of before choosing them, but we won't discuss them here.

ALTERNATIVE INVESTMENTS: *Options, Futures, FOREX, Gold, Real Estate, Etc. So, you now know about the two basic securities: equity and debt, better known as stocks and bonds. While many (if not most) investments fall into one of these two categories, there are numerous alternative vehicles, which represent the most complicated types of securities and investing strategies.*

The good news is that you probably don't need to worry about alternative investments at the start of your investing career. They are generally high-risk/high-reward securities that are much more speculative than plain old stocks and bonds. Yes, there is the opportunity for big profits, but they require some specialized knowledge. So, if you don't know what you are doing, you could get yourself into a lot of trouble. Experts and professionals generally agree that new investors should focus on building a financial foundation before speculating.

The following article from Investopekdia.com is one of the most simplified articles for beginners who are interested in deciding which type of investment vehicle(s) will be appropriate for their financial goals and objectives:

"Contrary to popular belief, there are actually two ways to make money from investing. First, most investors intend to buy at a low price and sell at a high price. This is popular with day traders, who expect to gain from short-term trends, and buy-and-hold investors, who anticipate the rise of profits and price of the stock of the company over a period of time. Second, many investors prefer a residual cash flow. They purchase stocks from businesses that yield dividends. Those businesses grow at a modest rate. Many individuals decide to go this route. Dividends may not be as aggressive as earnings from selling stock; however, the dividends are slightly more secure than to buy and hold. Even though many people view investing into companies a volatile market, stocks can be sold at any time, making it easy to sell. If you need your cash in a hurry or are not satisfied with the performance of your investment, you will always have an option to sell."

Here is another simple, yet informative article for beginners found on the advantages of investing in the stock market from TheNest.com:

High Return. Stocks are risky assets. This means they don't have a guaranteed return and sometimes lose money. However, the long-run trend of the stock market has been undeniably upward. Stocks have the highest return of any investment asset over the long term. According to the Federal Reserve, the stock market has grown by an average of more than 10 percent a year over the past 50 years. During this same period, government bonds only grew by 5 percent a year. If you can stomach the market swings, you will see the highest return on your money with the stock market.

*   ***Liquidity.** The stock market is a huge auction house. Every day, investors are buying and selling their shares. This makes stocks a liquid investment. When you want to cash out, it is quick and easy to find a buyer. Other assets are much more difficult to sell. If you invested in an investment property, it could take months to find a buyer and get your money out. With stocks, you can find a buyer the very next day.*

*   ***Delayed Taxation.** Stocks also delay taxation on your gains. If you buy a stock and it goes up in value, you don't need to file a return on the earnings. You only need to report your stock gains when you sell the shares for a profit. In addition, if you lost money on another stock purchase, you can use the loss to reduce taxes on your other stock gains. If you put your money in an investment that earns interest, like a bond or bank account, you need to pay tax on your earnings each year.*

*   ***Information.** The stock market is closely watched by the entire world. If a company wants to publicly sell its stock, it needs to release its financial statements that show how it is being run. The U.S. Securities and Exchange Commission reviews these statements to make sure they're true. In addition, financial reporters are reporting on stocks day and night. This makes it easy to research your stock*

investments. Some other investments do not have as much public information, so it is harder to make an informed decision.

Again, the stock market is just **one** of many potential places to invest your money to potentially build massive wealth. Investing can often be risky, which draws a response to the huge gains and losses of some investors. But if you manage the risks, you can seize the opportunistic reward of the stock market and secure your financial goal.

"There is no secret to being wealthy:
1) Fill up a ROTH IRA every year to its max of $5,500
or as close as you can.
2) Get a Term Life Insurance policy ASAP!
3) Buy one (1) stock monthly.
4) Check, Challenge, & Correct your credit report.
Lastly, my least favorite; invest into your 401K to the max."
~ Oliver Emerson ~

Become an entrepreneur and start a business. This ambiguous statement has such a vast nebulous of success that it takes almost a lifetime to articulate. There are many individuals who have found success through starting a business. Some individuals discover early in life that they were born to be an entrepreneur. Others discover later in life due to events in life (job layoff or termination, marriage, divorce, parenthood, sickness, retirement, etc.). No matter when the notion was discovered, it was discovered for a reason.

In the world of entrepreneurship, one of the greatest advantages it will offer is a five-letter word: **TAXES**. The United States government (through the Internal Revenue Service) has been and will forever be in favor of small businesses and those who plan to be a part of them. Small businesses are the backbone of the U.S. economy. Ever since the term *laissez faire* was introduced in 1681 between both French businessmen and finance ministers, the United States adopted the policy where transactions between private parties are free from government intervention in the free market. This means that the government must "let go" or relinquish full control over all private businesses. The government understands that, in order to further stimulate the economic growth of this country, it must be lenient with those who start businesses. Depending on the business, many expenses can be deducted from taxes such as food, a phone bill, travel and operating expenses, portions of mortgage and auto payments, etc. There are even government incentives for certain start-up businesses that qualify. Be sure to consult with an accountant about eligible deductions for your particular business. But one thing is almost certain; the average individual who owns their own business and makes 100K a year pays fewer taxes than an individual who works for an employer and makes 100K a year!

You also have an advantage of being your own boss. You are in complete control. The destiny of your business and financial future is now in your hands. You are now transitioning from an employee to self-employed. This demands a new way of thinking. You don't mind working more hours for your own business than your normal job. It's part of building your business. It belongs to you. It will not grow and expand unless you do the work. Sacrificing is a major part of growing your business. However, there will be much more rewards than sacrifices if you consistently stay the course of building it. The provision in the freedom of a flexible schedule will become one of the greatest rewards of having your own business.

There aren't many other accomplishing feeling moments than when you pursue your passion, create something brand new, set your own schedule and deadlines, call all the shots, create your own work environment, and write and sign all of the checks. Knowing that you are building to provide job security for yourself and potentially others is an accomplishment within itself. Not to mention the potential posterity of financial wealth that could be passed down to the next generation and generations to come. Leaving an inheritance and generational wealth is the average individual's dream and goal in life. This way of living takes focus, determination, drive, consistency, long-suffering, patience, and a will to never give up.

If you want to achieve financial success through starting a business, become disciplined and astutely skilled in your business.

This is a major proponent in building and acclimating wealth successfully as an entrepreneur. Award-winning Director, Producer, Entrepreneur, and Founder of Tyler Perry Studios, Tyler Perry discusses his *7 Key Habits to Financial Wealth'* (courtesy of Pinterest):

1. Make a plan and raise your standards.
2. Immediately, start a business and duplicate it worldwide.
3. Stop wasting your time on tv, games, dumb stuff, and people. If a person doesn't have a plan, move on.
4. Figure out a way to make $1,000, $2,000, then $5,000, etc..... weekly. Save 40% of whatever you earn and invest it!
5. Stop buying stuff that has no value. Cars, clothes, dumb jewelry, food, etc.
6. Educate yourself. **READ. READ. READ.** Read books on the greatest people. Learn something new daily.
7. Stop eating bad food. Eat organic only. Bad food changes your brain chemistry.

Invest in real estate. Real estate is arguably one of the best asset-building strategies if you want to build massive wealth. While you may have heard of real estate investor tycoons such as President Donald Trump or Rick Caruso, there are numerous others who are rather unknown, yet wealthy. China's Wang Jianlin, Hong Kong's Lee Shau Kee, and the U.S. native David Lichtenstein are just a few who are listed among Forbes' Top 100 Billionaires. Many of these investors prefer to live relatively insignificant lives in public. They understand that the real estate market is a promising way to achieve colossal financial success. There are at least six powerful tools these real estate tycoons were able to use to build legacy wealth from real estate. While most of these tools apply to both real estate investors and homeowners, there are more benefactors from owning real estate as an investor rather than a homeowner. A few listed are:

- Limited amount of real estate
- Tax benefits
- Cash flow
- Asset appreciation
- Leverage equity for more acquisition
- Amortization

Limited Supply. You can't produce more land, but more land produced more demand. There is a fixed supply of land and an aggregate demand for it. The world population is continuing to grow, but not land.

If you use the principle of supply and demand, a fixed supply of something with an aggregate demand causes prices to increase. This, combined with the essential need for people to live somewhere, guarantees a future demand for real estate.

"Buy land. They're not making it anymore."
~ Mark Twain ~

Tax benefits. Investing in real estate continues to be one of the best ways to acquire wealth and save on taxes. Benefits include the ability to recover the cost of income-producing property through depreciation, use of the IRS Code 1031 exchanges to defer profits from real estate investments, borrow against real estate, mortgage interest deduction, and other purposes. Additionally, homeowners can profit from the personal-residence exemption, which protects profits on the sale of a personal residence from capital gains taxes.

The best way to look at real estate is the same way you would for a business. Having a business provides that business with certain tax deductions. The tax incentives available to owners of real estate are available to persuade the owners to reinvest in the property to improve it. These tax benefits also persuade individuals to buy property, helping to increase the demand for home ownership.

Cash flow. If you are buying real estate as an asset, then cash flow is one of the profits you should consider to be at the top of your list. The term "Cash Flow" is the difference left over after you collect the rent and pay your mortgage, taxes, insurance, repairs, etc. and any other immediate liabilities. It is your money, revenue, and profit. Let's look at an example.

Envision with the purchase of your very first rental property, you cash-flowed $200 monthly. Now, imagine owning 25 of them. That's $5,000 monthly generated while you sleep. And, if you don't want to deal with the hustle and bustle of the daily management, you can contract an outside property management company that will handle the business of the property for a fee. That's great passive income! For the most part, the only thing left for you to do is collect and write checks. Now, of course, this is easier said than done—but the portrait has been painted. Rental properties are a property owner's best friend in this market. There are not many things much sweeter than to watch your income grow while you sleep because you have tenants who grow your business and make you money! It is not as stimulating as capital appreciation, but it is inevitably constant. And as inflation increases, your cash flow should, at the very least, remain constant each year. This means the passive income from real estate can be secured and hedged, even against inflation. The value of most primary assets is not depreciated by inflation. In fact, according to Robert Shiller, a Yale economist famously known for his Case-Shiller Home Price Index, real estate does well against inflation over long periods of time. It's not that they don't exist, but there aren't many other investments that have that type of revenue advantage.

Asset Appreciation. Fundamentally, asset appreciation is the growth of the value of the real estate. Over time, this is constant as long as inflation is consistent. Since real estate tends to keep pace with inflation, it is important for inflation to be existent. On the contrary, real estate prices do not always increase with inflation. But over the long term, an asset in real estate is going to appreciate and increase in value over time. Asset appreciation is the one inconsistency in real estate that cannot be predicted with absolute confidence. Periods of the historic housing crisis in the 20th and early 21st centuries have shown that it is not always the case. As an investor, some experts advise that appreciation should be considered as a gratuity, not strategy. Asset appreciation is wonderful, but not the goal being considered.

Leverage. Building wealth in real estate is one of the rare advantages where you can use massive amounts of leverage to own an asset, and banks will favorably afford it to you. Leverage, in basic terms, means to invest a small amount of your own money, and borrow the rest from a lender. Leverage is a way to enlarge the returns you receive on that asset, in both directions, being advantageous and risky. So, make sure it will work for you.

To buy a home, most lenders desire a 20% down payment of the purchase price in cash. If you are buying a $200,000 home, then this means your down payment will be $40,000 and you will mortgage $160,000. This provides you with 5x leverage. This means that if the value of your home goes up 2% from $200,000 to $204,000, then your equity in that home goes from $40,000 to $44,000. This is a 10% rise. **That's great!**

It is hard to imagine that a low 2% rise in the value of your asset can produce double-digit returns, but that is why leverage is a great tool for building wealth. Here is the disadvantage: It also works inversely. A 2% drop in the value of your home causes a 10% drop in your equity. The golden rule is not to use leverage unless the asset is appreciating.

Amortization. Here is another great benefiting component where your tenants play the major role. Let's configure. The most common type of mortgage loan is a 30-year fixed rate mortgage loan. It has a fixed interest rate that will remain constant for the full 30-year tenure of the loan. In the infant stage of the loan, most of your monthly payment is paid towards the interest on the loan rather than to principal. About halfway through the term (15 years), the dispersal of your payments between interest and principal should be about half and half. Therefore, the longer you hold the property, the more of the loan principal your tenants are paying down and the more wealth you are creating for yourself. This is where the term "buy and hold" is used. For example, you have a $200,000 bank loan with a monthly mortgage payment of $1,076. In year one, approximately $828 of this payment will go towards paying the interest, while $248 will go towards paying down the principal on the loan. Let's do the math:

$248 (monthly principal payment) x 12 (months)

= $2,976 (principal reduction for the year

****

$200,000 (mortgage loan)

— $2,976 (principal payments after year 1)

= $197,024 (loan balance after year 1)

By year 15, approximately $550 of the monthly mortgage payment will go towards interest, while the remaining $526 will be applied towards the principal.

$526 (monthly principal payment) x 12 (months)

= $6,312 (principal reduction for the year)

Every year that you own this property, the **tenants** are paying off your mortgage with **their** money. By reducing the amount of your mortgage, you are building equity in the property or wealth, being able to eventually access the equity either by refinancing your loan or by selling the property.

As the evidence shows, there are many rewards to real estate investing and ways to build wealth in real estate investing. With the proper education, mindset, and goals, real estate investing can be a top strategy to build a net worth for anyone. Now, before we end this section, let's clear the air before going further.

There is a popular myth that a real estate license is required to be a real estate investor. However, you do not need a real estate license to become a real estate investor. A real estate license is needed to SELL real estate using a bank, mortgage, or some other lending institution. So again: **YOU DO NOT NEED A REAL ESTATE LICENSE TO BECOME A REAL ESTATE INVESTOR.** No experience or license is needed; just a willing individual to put in the work and time to become successful.

"Buying real estate is not only the best way, the quickest way, the safest way, but the only way to become wealthy."

~ Marshall Field

FAITH

If you are single,

Be Grateful in the State You are In.

**You must understand that if you are single,
you are really blessed.**

Some of the most successful people in the world will all have this piece of advice to give you: Be grateful for where you are. But understand: You can also be appreciative and voracious concurrently. Being single **definitely** has its advantages and benefits. You have absolute time to get things in order. Keeping the expression and notion of gratitude for being single will challenge and change your philosophy on the atomic significance of being single. Being single is not just about preparing for marriage. It should also be about preparing for your best self, learning who you are, and your reason for being on this earth.

You are so much bigger than a spouse and a family.

You have so much more to offer this world and society. The world has so much more to offer you than a house and a white picket fence. You must expose yourself to all of the things you desire. They will not come to you. You must pursue them. You must transition in your mind from the philosophy that being single is a curse.

79

Being single should be a time in life where opportunity is at an all-time high for you. There are many married individuals who absolutely love their spouses faithfully; however, they wished they had capitalized their singleness and attained certain goals. They now understand that being single was not about finding their mate in life. They understand…

Being single is about finding your place in life.

Also, this is the period of life when you are free to make your own decisions. Whether if it is to wake up on your own time or deciding to take a last-minute trip out of the country, you do not have to consult with anyone. Arguments or disagreements won't be a problem. There are no obligations to check in. Your weekends are yours. Your time with family and friends isn't limited (unless by your discretion). Your money is your money. You have the freedom to develop needed relationships. You have the liberty and freedom to date by choice. You can relocate at any given time. You have the time to discover who you are. Being single is a time for growth and maturity. You can be as liberal at giving and philanthropy as you choose, and so much more. There are endless reasons to be grateful during your time of being single. To be single is a gift. To be married is a gift. You can't earn singleness and you can't earn marriage. Both require work within themselves to be successful in whichever one a person is in. Take advantage of every grateful reason to be single. When your time comes to espouse, you can enter knowing you fulfilled your time purposefully while being single.

"Be thankful for what you have; you'll end up having more.
If you concentrate on what you don't have,
you will never, ever have enough."
~ Oprah Winfrey ~

If you are single,

Give.

Knowledge is power. Power is influence. Influence is contagious.

There are many people who need what you have.

There are many people who need what you know.

Wisdom is applied knowledge. Knowledge is learned education. Education is taught instructions. Instructions are oral or written directives. Unless there is someone who is sharing their directives (oral or written), there will be no conversion from instructions to wisdom. Don't be afraid of sharing what you know or what you have to help aid or foster a person in becoming who they need to become. Truth be told, no one has gotten to the place where they wanted to be in life without the help of other individuals and their wisdom—**someone** gave to them and **someone** has given to *you*. Pass it on.

"Give, and it will be given to you. A good measure, pressed down, shaken together and running over, will be poured into your lap. For with the measure you use, it will be measured to you."

~ Holy Bible (NIV) ~

If you are single,

Spend Time with Your Family.

There are some moments that can't be replaced. There are some moments that can't be replayed. There are some moments that you can only get the maximum gratification only during your experience of it. Many times, those moments are with the family. Family members and the concept and substratum of the family cannot be replaced. It is the core of the history of mankind. As a matter-of-fact, according to Genesis 2 in the Bible, the procreation of mankind created the first family. This is important. Spend time with your family. Whether they are biological or adopted, embrace your family. An online article from SheKnows.com gives five healthy reasons why spending time with family is a must:

1. *Builds self-esteem in children*
2. *Strengthens family bonds*
3. *Develops positive behaviors*
4. *Creates happy memories*
5. *Helps parents and children reconnect*

It is said that a child's birthday party helps to significantly boost their self-esteem and increases their personal connection with the family. They can feel the genuine love and care from those around them and understand what love, giving, and appreciation sincerely is. When love is extended and received, endorphins are released, and a healthy chemical reaction occurs. This helps to positively balance the individual psychologically for a period of time to help and store healthy and happy memories, which is why family activities shouldn't be a scarcity. The more engagement of healthy family activities, the stronger the family bond. The bond helps the family endure hardships as a family to bring the family closer. A family like this can withstand the tests of time.

In addition, a stronger bond promotes communication among each other and decreases the chances of negative activity outside of the home. Did you know that youth whose parents discuss the adverse effect of sexual activity are more likely to practice abstinence? Did you know that youth whose fathers are involved in their education are more likely to have better grades? Did you know that fathers who are heavily involved in their daughters' lives significantly decrease psychological problems and depression in the daughters' lives from adolescence to womanhood? *Family* can bring about a healthy balance to an individual's life that will leave a lasting impression of strength and stability.

Spending adequate time with family and friends also helps to develop a healthy relationship with a spouse or significant other. This is a factor that many individuals look for when selecting a stable mate. When it's not the time for romance, it's time to be a friend, teammate, or partner. When it's not the time for friendship, this may be a time to be closer to that person than their family. Having a healthy relationship with your family can teach how to overcome obstacles, forgive when offended or wounded, and love unconditionally in a monogamous relationship. These factors are essential and necessary when desiring a healthy, intimate relationship with a mate. Love yourself, love your family, and love your mate.

"Family is not an important thing. It's everything."

~ Michael J. Fox ~

If you are single,

Practice Celibacy.

W ith the influx of the diversity and disposal of technology and mass media that focuses on imagery or propaganda related to human sexuality, many industries use sexuality as a ploy to quickly draw attention to their agendas and objectives. It is used to bring more viewers to a particular visual program, sell products and intellectual property, or bring awareness to a particular subject. In other words, it is vastly known that *"Sex Sells"*. However, it is scarcely heard or seen that *"Celibacy Sells"*, too. This is because there is very little information broadcasted about the positive facets of celibacy. For many individuals, to live a celibate life is to live the best life. The Dalai Lama, one of the most respected and admired leaders in the world, once said the following pertaining to sex:

"Naturally as a human being...some kind of desire for sex comes, but then you use human intelligence to make comprehension that those relationships are always full of trouble. Sexual pressure, sexual desire, actually, I think is short-period satisfaction and, often, that leads to more complications."

There is a plethora of beneficial reasons to practice celibacy. Here are some of the most commonly-known reasons many people do:

- To avoid all Sexually-Transmitted Diseases
- To avoid an unplanned pregnancy or abortion
- To avoid the possibility of becoming a sex addict or pornography addict
- To experience less mental and emotional attachment to a single person
- To make sound, unclouded judgments and decisions regarding an intimate relationship
- To recognize the difference between sex and love
- To realize love is not partial to romantic connections

The reasons listed above are legitimately genuine reasons why many people abstain from sexual activity. However, there are some spiritual reasons individuals have discovered but many haven't considered that it will help in a person's totality. An article from Beliefnet.com discusses five spiritual benefits of abstinence and celibacy that have been turning points for many individuals:

Learn Self-Control

More than on a physical level, we battle with self-control when it comes to our emotions. Practicing abstinence allows us to develop more patience as we are less inhibited to act out in an irrational manner.

Balanced Relationships

Instead of focusing on the sexual aspect of a relationship, we have the time to better cultivate our personal relationships. There is more thought and a deeper connection with a significant other or friend.

Decreased Health Risks

No sex means less likely to contract sexually-transmitted diseases (STD's). It also removes the pressure of an unwanted pregnancy. Studies show that abstaining from sexual activity can also boost your immune system and improve your memory.

Patience for the Right Relationship

There are less worries and stress on jumping into a relationship before you are ready. You take the time to get to know and love yourself, and your boundaries. When the right person or relationship comes your way, you can get to know them without any pressure.

Inner-Confidence and Peace

Abstinence is more than just a halt on sex, but an emotional and spiritual journey. You can gain peace of mind, joy, and a confidence you may not have had before.

Celibacy also keeps intimate dominion over your body in your possession. Any time you give away or transfer your possession of intimacy into the hands of another person, you lose the power to completely govern and control it. That is why it is better to abstain until marriage if you're going to be sexually active. When you are sexually active in marriage, you don't lose your control because you and your spouse are joined and are considered as one individual.

Celibacy presents many facets to aid an individual in developing a rich totality. Some may consider it the best tool for health and spiritual progress. Some individuals also discover and learn their best "self" during this period of life. Through the eyes of the media and society, the celibate lifestyle is shunned. However, many have discovered the blissful peace it brings to life and the protection of being safe rather than sorry.

"I believe that abstinence is a response on the outside to what's going on; celibacy is a response from the inside. It should be a period of clarity, confidence, security, and empowerment that you give to yourself first."
~ Marcia Alene ~

If you are single,

Develop a Close Relationship with God.

This is the absolute most important awakening to express and impress in this entire book. This should be your first action (if not already established). Various psychological studies have concluded that a child's relationship with his or her father has a big impact on success in his or her life. Reported benefits of a good father-child relationship include improved stress response, higher academic success, lower levels of aggression and depression, and greater ability to make and keep intimate relationships as an adult. It is the same concept with a relationship with God—and an intimate relationship with Him has the **BEST** advantages as well. Highlighted here are advantages of having a close relationship with God:

- **God wants to shower you with blessings, benefits, and advantages.** Good fathers want to give their children advantages in life, and God is the preeminent Father. He loves you so much that He wants you to be His child and to have the absolute best. God wants you to have a relationship with Him because He *made* you to have a relationship with Him. He wants you to love Him because He loves you unconditionally. By learning the way He loves you, you learn to love others the same way. There is nothing you can do to earn God's love. It's freely given, and it is given to you so you can give it to others. He promises that when we give our lives to Him, He is always with us—even in the darkest times of our lives. Even in times of trouble, call on Him and He will rescue you.

- **God also wants you to have a home in Heaven.** He has a place just for you. It is reserved for you with your name on it. His Son, Jesus, has prepared a special place in Heaven for you. Living on the earth is one of the greatest gifts God has granted mankind. However, absolutely nothing will be greater than achieving eternal life. That is the ultimate prize God will reward His people who enter Heaven. You must accept His Son, Jesus Christ, as Lord over your life to live the best life possible and inherit the ultimate reward: **ETERNAL LIFE.**

- **Not only does He want you to have eternal life, but to live the best life on earth.** Through His Spirit, He wants to give you a life filled with abundance and blessings. He wants to give you not just tangible gifts, but gifts that come directly from Him: Spiritual Gifts—gifts that are so valuable, they cannot be measured. Gifts such as love, joy, peace, patience, kindness, goodness, faithfulness, gentleness, and self-control. These gifts cannot be purchased from Him, only given from Him. The Holy Spirit—*perhaps the best gift He gives us all*—personally guides, leads, and equips us to live the best life. He desires to dwell in you to assist in your transformation of life to live as Christ lived: empowered, inspired, and enlightened.

The Holy Spirit will help you overcome and conquer any challenges, mountains, and extremities that life brings. There is no single thing too hard that God's Holy Spirit cannot help you defeat. All things become subject to God through His Son, Jesus Christ. It is through Christ that mankind is able to have the best relationship with our Great God!

- **God also has the perfect plan and purpose for your life.** His plans for you are so awesome and great! They exceed your highest expectations, goals, and objectives for your life. Ask Him and seek what His plans are for your life, and He will amaze you with them. His plans will always be to bless you and not to harm you whatsoever. He is filled with love and compassion, and His purposes for your life will be centered around them. It is **HE** who fulfills His purposes in us.

- **God wants to free you from the guilt and shame of your past and present faults.** He wants you to experience life through His eyes. He wants you to see what He sees so you can do what He does. But in order to do so, you must be free from all things that cloud your vision. That includes all guilt, shame, wrong decisions, mistakes, and things that bring division between you and His Spirit. He has to and wants to forgive you for all of those things in order for you to live the most prosperous life. Ask Him for His forgiveness for your mistakes and wrong decisions. He is such a **GREAT** God that He will take the things that made us guilty and shameful and use them to bless us.

Following is a great corresponding article from Karen T. Hluchan from Patch.com:

Mistakes can be Beneficial

"As we live our lives every day, God lovingly watches over us. He knows the paths our lives are taking and the effects of the choices we make, as well as the best way for us to go. He sees when we deviate from that path. He exerts His power with a loving hand to guide us back to the paths that are in line with our soul plans. As a spirit in human form, we become frustrated when we see ourselves or others going down a path that will ultimately cause more pain. With God, He views our errors and mistakes as learning lessons. It is beneficial for us to view our setbacks and missteps in the same way. God extends great love and compassion toward our souls. We give ourselves the greatest gift of kindness and love when we extend the same courtesy toward ourselves and others."

"It's not about religion; it's about relationship."

~ R. Allan Woods ~

Conclusion

In conclusion, I hope you have been inspired to maximize every moment of your life and fulfill every purpose and goal you plan to accomplish. Whether you are single or married, just know there is more to life than your paradigm. You were created to create and dominate, not just accept and adapt. Grab the horns of your life and command it to run in **YOUR** direction, not its own. Your greatest opportunity is here because your only opportunity is *NOW*.

Tomorrow is not promised. You are **READY**. You are **SET**. Now, **GO**!

References

http://www.huffingtonpost.com/shannon-kaiser/3-unexpected-ways-to-find_b_5176511.html

https://www.nytimes.com/2015/05/17/travel/travel-industry-responds-to-rise-in-solo-sojourners.html?_r=0

http://nextshark.com/10-reasons-why-successful-people-under-30-stay-single/

http://www.tradingeconomics.com/united-states/consumer-spending

http://blog.iqmatrix.com/a-life-of-excuses

http://www.inc.com/peter-economy/7-keys-becoming-effective-manager.html

http://www.dictionary.com/browse/homeostasis

http://www.gallup.com/businessjournal/191852/millennials-likely-shop-fun-impulse.aspx

https://www.forbes.com/sites/learnvest/2017/02/17/credit-scores-vs-credit-reports-whats-the-difference/#2d92781235ed

https://www.fha.com/fha_credit_requirements

http://www.investopedia.com/university/beginner/beginner5.asp

http://budgeting.thenest.com/types-personal-investments-20558.html

https://www.pinterest.com/pin/544091198710830829/

http://www.sheknows.com/parenting/articles/831061/5-reasons-family-time-rocks

http://www.beliefnet.com/wellness/galleries/5-benefits-of-abstinence-that-you-probably-havent-considered.aspx

http://patch.com/pennsylvania/horsham/the-benefits-of-building-a-strong-relationship-with-god

About the Author

A prolific preacher, millennial leader, visionary, creator, and father, Louis The PreachR is a horn to the generation of young adults. However, Louis is nowhere near your "ordinary" clergy. Chosen to be a 'Trumpet Voice', his mission is to change the trajectory of young adults (single and married) to live their God-given, purpose-filled lives through diverse cultural and social revolutions.

Inspired by God to maximize every moment and opportunity in life, Louis lives by and shares his philosophy: **"Be Authentic, Be Awesome, Be All."** He affirms:

"Out of my experience of being single my entire life, God has taught me that being single is one of the most fertile times of life to maximize my experiences and learn precisely who I am. I just want to share my truth with the world."